His Mistress, Her Muse
Poetry • Photography

Sensual

Erotic

Provocative

Monica Diane Zonni

Copyright 2025
Monica Diane Zonni

His Mistress, Her Muse
Poetry * Photography

All Rights Reserved

No text or images in this book may be used
or reproduced in any manner without
written permission of Monica Diane Zonni.

All the photographs in the book were taken by
Monica Diane Zonni in St. Augustine, Florida.
Most were taken in the Fullerwood neighborhood.

ISBN: 979-8-9893938-7-9

Cover Design and Interior Layout by Ashley Coursey

Published by Legacies & Memories
Legacies & Memories, LLC
St. Augustine, Florida

LegaciesandMemories.com
LegaciesandMemoriesPublishing.com

*Memories are made up of small truths churning
in an ocean of misconceptions, skewed perceptions,
dashed hopes, ludicrous dreams, unabashed emotions
and manic desires, momentarily rising and dipping
below the choppy surface of one's mind.*

Monica Diane Zonni

Dedication

To he who is handsome and born of fire

Contents

Epigraph
Dedication

SWEETWATER PREMONITION...11

SAMHAIN...13

ANTICIPATION...15

FEAST...17

CASINO...19

SYNOPSIS...21

RETRIBUTION...23

IN NEED OF PENANCE...25

BUZZED...27

SUFFOCATING...29

LOVER/AMANTE...31

SACRIFICE...33

BLESSED...35

HIBERNATE...37

A HAPPY ENDING...39

FREED...41

VCR...43

PROMISE...45

ECHO...47

WISDOM...49

INSPIRED...51

CHAINED...53

DESPAIR...55

LOVE LETTER...57

YOUR WISH...59

SECRET...61

TOGETHER WE DROWN...63

ALCHEMY...65

I DESIRE...67

SELFIE...69

CHEST...71

About Monica Diane Zonni...73

His Mistress, Her Muse
Poetry • Photography

SWEETWATER PREMONITION

crystal clear warmth washes past my skin
I am submerged in the spring trembling
how far does the water flow from within
how ancient is this love I am remembering

the depth from which this life force pumps
a distance traveled through time and space
coursing, seeking, defying gravity, it jumps
softly licking, like wet kisses on my face

SAMHAIN

today it was as if
I could taste your kiss still
a creole spell on my lips
carried back to me on the wind
now in my memory I recall
a fire repeatedly stoked
fueled by intense desires
sultry whispers you spoke
breathing me in more
expand, rise and release
magic into my portal

ANTICIPATION

my desire feels like a ravenous animal

pacing frantically inside my ribcage

consequently time cannot pass but stills

seconds masquerade as lifetimes

every possible scenario plays on a loop

eyes, fingers, lips, thighs, tongues, sighs

FEAST

the universe sees intention in time
my lover will fill me with his sum
this hidden union is not a crime
it is the purest pleasure, like the sun
my entire body is covered sublime
sweet and tasty he feeds on my plum
I am glowing as a goddess divine
he will return soon to me at full run
I wait fully spread for him to dine
a promise of our bodies becoming one

CASINO

it was best you were lyfted away
I was a little dizzy once I stood
I returned to the sheets of play
I luxuriated in the hopes of could

it seemed all my energies slept
I felt unable to gather strength
I am the gambler who placed a bet
I rationalize hope to what lengths

it has to be viewed only one way
I had slipped into an alternate reality
I have nothing to justify or truly say
I will cast the dice and wait and see

SYNOPSIS

silly things said
intense stories shared
revealing healed scars
joining our bodies
a sensuous secret

RETRIBUTION

at first my eyes drank in
the details of your face
coveting became my sin
forgetting you my place

recently the universe gave
a chance kiss among fire
each lip's motion to save
rekindling embers of desire

IN NEED OF PENANCE

do I share myself too much
in the space of separation
betwixt this lush hush hush
you reign my concentration

perhaps it's the memories
shadowing me in my bed
igniting dirty little fantasies
that can't help but be said

my fingers mimic your tongue
I slowly explore in delicate trace
imagining you immensely sprung
deep inside of me slowing pace

throbbing, stiff, beyond hard
acts so delish like confections
everything manifesting by bard
I pulse and drip my confessions

BUZZED

every cell inside of me is humming silently
a muted gong ripples and shakes my body
I sit still moved by a symphony within
the chords are the rhythms of you honey

it is somehow tied to the breeze outside
connected to the pulsing rays of the sun
in sync with the eruptions of earth's lava
I am lulled listening to this perfection sung

SUFFOCATING

your touch is
like needed oxygen
and I don't know
how much longer
I can go without
breathing you in

LOVER/AMANTE

lover…how long have I waited for you?
some do say, since the creation of stars
I say, since light first radiated its beam
lover…how long will I worship you?
some do say, after stars cease to burn
I say, beyond each galaxy's last breath

amante...per quanto tempo ti ho aspettato?
alcuni dicono, dalla creazione delle stelle
Io dico, da quando la luce ha irradio per la
prima volta il suo raggio
amante...per quanto tempo ti adorerò?
alcuni dicono, dopo che le stelle cesseranno
di bruciare
Io dico, oltre l'ultimo respiro di ogni galassia

SACRIFICE

in this life I am an all or nothing girl
possessing love and wisdom's pearl
enough time has passed to give sight
destiny calls us to a passionate flight
these paths we forge and must take
decisions made for future realities sake

BLESSED

I recognize divine presence within you
a stardust crystal rainbow of every hue
purest vibration our energies require
fueling earthly bodies' burning desire
entwined we become oiled and spiced
my body slick, entangled and sacrificed
your touch embalms and mummifies me
entombed in this passion forever I'll be

HIBERNATE

as the skies gray and the leaves fall
our bodies slow and our senses dull
we become in sync with winter's pulse
to do otherwise would be utterly false

draw inward to release what has died
your core still vibrant, exterior dried
relish this sleepy trance falling deep
in tandem with the earth's time to sleep

tonight a full wolf moon will surely rise
time to swell intentions into the skies
mantra to sow desires as seeds spoken
all will be healed and no longer broken

A HAPPY ENDING

penned deep into my bed
I replayed all of it in my head
tenderness spoken and said
empty places filled and fed
the past vanished and fled
hearts no longer being bled
our bodies magically led
a story not written yet read

FREED

I am both angel and animal for you
pure, ethereal with unbridled power
your tongue lashes and tames me
lapping my heavenly nectar's flower
your keen eyes pin me into submission
onto my knees in a pleasurable cower
your every inch fills my hungry mouth
imprisoned externally on an erect tower
your tender touch traces finding wings
my senses fly firing like a meteor shower
your kisses delicate, deep and delicious
prayer on my lips spoken hour after hour
your muscled form engulfs my curves
I am protected, laid, hidden in a bower
your arrow penetrates taking away flight
time after time, snared by you, my fowler

VCR

visiting my house
creating sultry reels
resting in bedroom

you are so kind
please rewind

PROMISE

I slid between covers infused with our coupling

I couldn't bear to strip the bed, to begin canceling

I needed to soak up the remnants of us exchanging

I sought the feel and memories therein of commingling

I switched your pillow for my own, deeply inhaling

I was transported into your calm embrace remembering

I writhed trying to recapture you inside me cuming

I realized this can be more than what it is seeming

I felt my heart soaring, pounding, full of healing

I closed my eyes dreaming of a future meeting

ECHO

I woke up this dawn to the strangest sounds
a faint siren's wail, soon I did realize
notes sprang from the hollows of my womb
a cacophony of more dins joined in
every cell in my body sang in unison
as the shadow of kisses you left behind
was essence escaping as song from my lips

WISDOM

every human holds the key to their own heart
all the love that will ever be experienced by them
is made there and felt within its walls
when two hearts have the rare occasion
to sync up in rhythmic beats
either through a family, friendship or by intimate connection
they are blessed to experience feeling
the same pounding, mirrored back
when this happens a euphoric magic transpires, that is eternal
forever being felt and heard in the universe

you are full of love, as am I…

thank you for the time shared
where we flowed in this percussion of passion
adding to the music of life's sweetest symphony

INSPIRED

I am not wise in the ways of charting stars
nor am I versed in navigating the waves
I am a vessel in a world of the ocean seas
and you have appeared as a captain dear
a few others have tried to man the stern
pretending to be noble or to have strength
they selfishly set their own courses
without nurturing sails or oiling my deck
I have been abandoned on distant shores
I have slipped away fast when a tide arose
I have solace and peace in the emptiness
I do dream of the trees I once was part of
I do dream of destinations I desire to see
I do dream of your touch that I have known
captain of my bow and hull, command me
in all my years of unworthy commanders
of sloppy sailors feigning true knowledge
only with your battening, have I felt safe
in just a few leagues, you took me tenderly
guiding me into ports with such expertise
I rock back and forth in the peaceful bay
away from me you have ventured for now
oh captain, in faith I wait, hoping a return

CHAINED

I am choking, sobbing, gasping really
remembering a declaration by you spoken
to learn to drive the inner engine within me
not realizing that I am assuredly broken
I desire to extinguish fears and my anxiety
releasing to your hot passion, soaking it in
my body will not allow casual vulnerability
I dream of fluidity, but instead I am oaken
when you first entered, I was almost free
then past demons had once more awoken
I wish I could begin again to let myself be
abandoning entirely to your manly token
ecstasy with repetition, the only way for me
in time, the possibilities always do open
as I want innocently to climax with thee
believing in purity, forging a bond golden

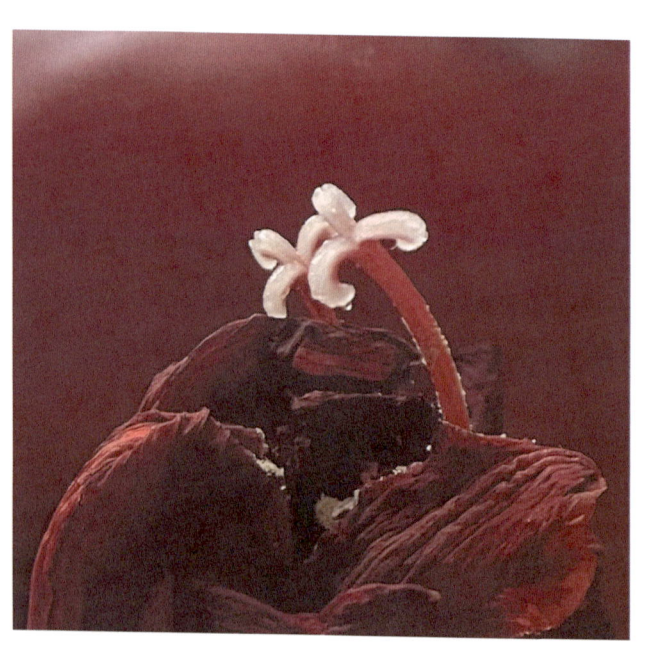

DESPAIR

as the days pass, distance dictated a decree
to form spaces between my thoughts of you
only the opposite occurs and I am taking a knee
oh lover, my heart is heavy with the color blue
when I close my eyes, it is only you that I see
every moment of the pleasures that we knew
playing over in my mind copulating to fly free
my stomach lurches as I stumble on worn shoe
I have become clumsy, my attitude is putrid tragedy
lover, oh my lover are you submerged so low too?

LOVE LETTER

I write this proclamation
of my feelings to the first
woman who loved you
it is she who shaped your
precious tiny heart in strength
that began to beat your life's song
within her sacred revered womb
it is she who nurtured you
and showed you tenderness
in turn you have this gift
I offer my deepest gratitude
to your exceptional mother
next my eternal thanksgiving
I must shower onto every lover
who taught you how to be
even the ones who only took
for you sir were the utmost
exquisitely made lover for me

YOUR WISH

happiness is a garden inside of me
love is the light that nourishes its soil
I am the gardener who tends the seed
its bounty must not rely on others toil

I nourish them well through meditation
like fertilizer certain people help growth
the burst of flourish is quite a sensation
as certain experiences can enhance both

yet it is I who is solely responsible here
opening up to the power of divine source
flowers blooming with inner faith not fear
fruit growing through my self-caring force

SECRET

did I think the realization and acceptance
of our shared limitations would somehow
cure my fever of lust?

that the trembles I feel when I think of you
would somehow cease to shake my core?

that I would stop remembering the feel
and the taste of you in my mouth?

my god! how smooth you felt on my tongue!

that my womb would magically stop
aching for the whole of you, lover?

so hard, hot and pumping into me
more and more…

no, I believe not, we exist now once again
as part of a circle of friends, yet hidden
within my sacred spaces, I will forever be
alight with this desire for you…

TOGETHER WE DROWN

I thought the sensations of not knowing
were all consuming, a volley of intense
longing, exhilarating anticipation, firing in
my mind and cunt in rapid succession fantasies

the next possible sight of you, how would
you then, lean in to place your lips to mine
and how would it feel when our naked bodies entwined
once more desiring an orgasm in unison

I realize now how intense are the feelings
of knowing that all has been consumed,
this current ripple of brutal force, drowning me,
in tempting waves of choking memories

the strike of lightning the first time we met,
the melding of our lips as our mouths first kissed,
the feel as you tenderly touched my hand last,
just before you closed the car door…

ALCHEMY

the truth is…

whether you are aware of it
or you were in control of it
whether you feel worthy of it
or felt you had the power to do it

you have been an alchemist for me
I am now changed and transformed
into a precious state of being

it began deep inside of myself
an invisible purity that is spreading
physically altering the whole of me

whether you will believe it
or could ever have dreamed it
whether you can now conceive of it
or will gain the ability to feel it

the truth of it is, what it is…

I DESIRE

the taste of tobacco laced saliva
the visual as it drips on my godiva
the feel as you gently split my fruit
the firm pulse of your magical flute
the words whispered into my ears
the way your voice banished fears
the movements as our bodies coil
the heat as our juices begin to boil
the precision of your hand's touch
the sensation of quiver and clutch
the explosion of the fill and release
the sleep of sweat soaked sheets

SELFIE

there it was, instantly brilliant, a yellow treat
this gifted message from the universe via uber
loosely covering such a perfected underneath
to any other eye, this pic would be a blooper

CHEST

before I knew you, I lacked nothing
my days were filled watching the trees
as they blossomed in green canopies
soaking in the sight of birds flocking
beating their wings upon landing
on the thin limbs bringing me to tears

before I knew you, my nights were complete
with the breathy dreams of imagining
all the wonderful and varying possibilities
and my arms would constantly be filled
with the child I once carried in my womb
always eager to be snuggled back to sleep

before I knew you, the work I did satisfied
with long fulfilled hours exchanging
varied simple rituals for deep raw truths
and all my free time was spent frolicking
with friends whom are imperfect but present
giving of their love in an endless dance

now that I know you, I have multiplied bliss
everything I had has become so much more
even in your absence I am overflowing
from a source of unworldly absolute knowing
for you are with me in every smile and heartbeat
part of every songs melody, as hidden treasure for me

About
Monica Diane Zonni

Monica Diane Zonni is a writer, photographer and business owner who featured more than 100 artists in her salon. Every artist was given a month to display their art, and Monica hosted an art opening monthly showcasing the artist to the community during the nine years she owned HEAD salonemporium, Inc., an Art Gallery/Salon in St. Augustine, Florida.

"My family for generations has been artists. For three years in the early 1900s, my Great Grandmother Clara H. Goetting attended The New York School of Applied Arts and Design for Women, which was at 23rd Street in Manhattan.

"My mother and one of my sisters are both painters and have dabbled in jewelry making. My oldest sister is a published author and university professor. She helped my father write a book that he self- published.

"My father is also a stylist and entrepreneur who used his artistic creativity in all his 19 business endeavors. When I was 12, he took me to Europe for three months and introduced me to the great art in Europe. This experience and exposure birthed my dream of wanting to own an art gallery, but I couldn't draw to save my life.

"In college, I teamed up with Jim Quine as his assistant for his photography business. That's when I fell in love with photography, and I also worked with Angela Biggs for many years. We even collaborated on a short film that got accepted into the Florida Film Festival presented by the Enzian Theatre in Orlando, Florida. I was her model and dabbled taking photos for myself with an old film camera that belonged to my great uncle.

"In the summer of 2009, I came up with the concept of a salon/gallery where I would be the performing artist hairstylist in a gallery setting. I made that dream come to fruition in the summer of 2012 with HEAD salonemporium, Inc. Since then, I have opened another salon where the business model does not support that same concept.

"With this new era of AI threatening all of our creativity, I feel more compelled than ever to produce original art from the human experience as seen and felt with the entirety of my organic being. I am vehemently against the use of AI in any way shape or form in the production of Art."

www.ingramcontent.com/pod-product-compliance
Lightning Source LLC
LaVergne TN
LVRC090726070526
838199LV00043B/743